Song and Dance

BOOKS BY ALAN SHAPIRO

Poetry

After the Digging

The Courtesy

Happy Hour

Covenant

Mixed Company

Selected Poems, 1974–1996

The Dead Alive and Busy

Song and Dance

Prose

In Praise of the Impure:
Poetry and the Ethical Imagination

The Last Happy Occasion

Vigil

Translation

The Oresteia by Aeschylus

Song and Dance

Alan Shapiro

A MARINER BOOK

Houghton Mifflin Company

Boston · New York

First Mariner Books edition 2004

For information about permission to reproduce selections
from this book, write to Permissions, Houghton Mifflin Company,
215 Park Avenue South, New York, New York 10003.

Visit our Web site: www.houghtonmifflinbooks.com.

Library of Congress Cataloging-in-Publication Data
Shapiro, Alan, date.
Song and dance / Alan Shapiro.
p.   cm.
ISBN 0-618-15285-7
ISBN 0-618-38229-1 (pbk.)
I. Title.
PS3569.H338 s6 2002
811'.54 — dc21   2001039527

Printed in the United States of America

WOZ 10 9 8 7 6 5 4 3 2 1

Design by Melissa Lotfy
Typefaces: Granjon, Spectrum

Grateful acknowledgment is made to the following publications, in
which these poems originally appeared: *Greensboro Review:* "The
Match." *Pedestal:* "If I Only Knew Then," "The Old Man." *Slate:*
"Scan," "The Phone Call," "The Accident." *Threepenny Review:*
"Broadway Revival." *Tikkun:* "Joy."

This book was greatly aided by a fellowship from the Project on
Death in America of the Open Society Institute and by a fellowship
term at the University of North Carolina's Institute for the Arts and
Humanities.

For Ellen, Arana and Rachel
Angels of Mercy

In memory of
David Eric Shapiro

Contents

Song and Dance

In class I said how the poem tied together an otherwise obtuse work. It has the feel the heavy hand significance of an ending. Shapiro placed this work, a natural final piece for a collection, at the beginning instead to pay homage to his siblings, who had bright memorable beginnings, once on which he wanted to focus his memory.

· Is his sister pretending to be Ethel Merman? Or is it their friend, who is named Ethel Merman

· She is no part of the real world, just an image we see as shadows capture our brains

    — but [see first two lines] — the boys are just poetry too — foretells his brother's death too — does he acknowledge his own, or is he just as insignificant to the "real" world as if he were dead?

Everything the Traffic Will Allow

The two boys don't suspect
                    they don't exist.
And Ethel Merman is
                    the shade of a shade
what Plato says
                    all poetry is —
                         a record
spinning beneath
                    a needle
                         as the boys
lip-sync into
           imaginary mikes
her glottal swagger,
                    brassy, large,
                              streetwise
and from their mouths
                    so touchingly naive
for being so . . .
           There's no
                    people
                         like show
                              people . . .
Their parents clap
                    and whistle
                         from the bed,
propped up
           on pillows . . .
                    Everything about

1

it is appealing . . .
They are shouting "Encore!
Bravo!"
when the boys,
like chorus girls,
arms on each other's shoulders,
step-kick their way
across the room
and out of it,
then back . . .
stealing that extra bow . . .
[Shades of a shade.
What poetry is.]
Because there's nowhere else
for them to be
except
inside the room
in which it isn't
when it is,
in which
there is no room
unless I think of it —

the boys
their arms flung wide
on one knee
mouthing the last words
before the needle slides

wonderful
four lines

2

off into silence,

   the parents propped up

      on pillows,

half laughing, half

    shouting "Bravo!

      Encore!"

        All now

just the shade

   of a shade —

      like no

       people

        I know . . .

[handwritten annotations:]

this is the key to the poem

Plato's cave allegory — everything we experience is just a shadow of truth

- Kilgore: there's no people like sho- people... everything about it is appealing... stealing that extra bow... like no people I know

hopefully this a/a couple of songs... it will make sense

Transistor Radio

Far down the beach
the roller coaster rippled in the heat haze

like a curvy bright
white trellis carved from cloud that a faint breeze

would scatter, though it held
somehow, somehow seemed more impalpable

for having held, for not
dispersing when the train of black cars

inched up the airy hill
of it to plunge down suddenly with a speed

that from far away looked slow
as reverie. How old was I? Free

for an hour from my weekend charge,
my traveling "companion" — my grandmother

he's alive. Where are siblings?
One dead, are dying?

alone at her rich brother's
beach house, with the shades drawn, the doors locked,

the bloated, stroke-crippled
indigent body hobbling from bed

to kitchen, kitchen to bed,
chain-smoking, muttering curses against her daughter,

her ex-husbands, against the cold
heart of a grandson who could just walk out

on her like that, too far
gone in her head to care about or notice

the trail of piss or shit
she left behind her always wherever she went,

→ are parents busy w/ the
other kids' predicaments

which it was my job
to clean up. Why I was made to come. The beach

was beautiful with bodies,
far off among the lazy swells, or strolling

to and from the surf,
or lounging all around me on sides, backs, bellies,

like a vast lair
of languid animals, or young gods stretching

and turning over, rubbing
themselves or each other with creams and lotions

up and down already
gleaming arms and shoulders, calves and thighs.

Inside my head the shit
trail, the piss trail, the stench, the ceaseless muttering.

Outside me, though, salt air,
fragrant oils, and the ever-shifting zones

of tinny croonings that
got louder and softer at the same time

as I wandered out among them,
down the beach, away from her, my every stride

delivering a new song
or the same song, each one another letter

in my new alphabet
of feeling. *Somewhere beyond the sea, somewhere . . .*

They were all so beautiful,
the boys and girls. *Dream lover, until then . . .*

Their bodies sang themselves.
They sang, *Come softly, darling, come to me, stay.*

It was so easy to.
So easy to forget. To keep on walking.

Your little hand in mine . . .
The beach went on and on. There was no end

to it —*My heart was flying* —
the massive bright white trellis that no white

was ever whiter than —
the way it rippled in the heat and held

so airily together
when the cars plunged over and the boys stood up

in the free fall waving
while the girls beside them shrieked the whole way down.

is he thinking of his brother & sister

"every stride..." these were 5 stanzas happen over the course of 5 steps

Sleet

What was it like before the doctor got there?

Till then, we were in the back seat of the warm
dark bubble of the old Buick. We were where
we'd never not been, no matter where we were.

And when the doctor got there?

Everything outside was in a rage of wind and sleet,
we were children, brothers, safe in the back seat,
for once not fighting, just listening, watching the storm.

Weren't you afraid that something bad might happen?

Our father held the wheel with just two fingers
even though the car skidded and fishtailed
and the chains clanged raggedly over ice and asphalt.

Weren't you afraid at all?

Dad sang for someone to fly him to the moon,
to let him play among the stars, while Mom
held up the lighter to another Marlboro.

But when the doctor started speaking . . .

The tip of the Marlboro was a bright red star.
Her lips pursed and she released a ring of Saturn,
which dissolved as we caught at it, as my dad sang Mars.

When you realized what the doctor was saying . . .

They were closer to the storm in the front seat.
The high beams, weak as steam against the walled swirling,
only illuminated what we couldn't see.

When he described it, the tumor in the brain and what it meant . . .

See, we were children. Then we weren't. Or my brother wasn't.
He was driving now, he gripped the steering wheel
with both hands and stared hard at the panicked wipers.

What did you feel?

Just sleet, the slick road, the car going way too fast,
no brother beside me in the back seat, no singing father,
no mother, no ring of Saturn to catch at as it floats.

itelly cos
Sister or brother asking about when the brother/sister
got sick (did one die before the other, or while
the other was young enough to not fully remember

· guidance counsler
  · sorting through it w/ him
· bully
  too slow + methodical

9

Scan

I wanted to watch the game.
The small room strewn

with magazines was too dark
to read in, lightless

but for the frenzied pulsing
of the muted screen

above the door, and for the
door, which a nurse would open

now and again onto
a blazing corridor

that this one's wife or that
one's son, when called, would leave for,

or drift back from, dazed
either way, coming

or going, by the light
first, then the dark.

I wanted to watch the game,
I could tell that time

was running out by how
the white team, spreading

the court, touch-passed
the ball from corner to key

to corner so quickly that
the yellow team couldn't

get close enough to foul,
the ball sailing just

beyond their reach as they lunged
for it, scrambled and dove,

frenetic, hopeless, in a
dumb-show of defeat.

I wanted to watch it, but
the lady next to me,

soon as my brother's name
was called, was telling me

"the story," what we all share,
our bond, our lingua franca,

the before, the after, signs
now unmistakable

but at the time ignored
until the stroke, or seizure.

I wanted to watch the game.
I wanted to tell the lady,

Lady, I don't know how long
my brother has to live,

my sister's dead, my parents
are dying, can't you just let

me watch the game in peace?
But the automatic iron

gears of courtesy
engaged, and I was just

so many different engines
of attention: a nameless friend,

a confessor, an innocent
who can't have any idea

of what it's like to live
with someone you've spent your life with

and see him this way, unable
to feel emotion, like a

well-trained zombie,
because that's what the tumor

damaged, where the feelings
come from in the brain.

My goodness, you must think
it's so selfish of me

to complain like this. I should
feel grateful, shouldn't I?

I mean, I know he has
no sense of what we're all

going through for him,
and so he can't really

love us now, not me, not → grandchildren
even the children. But at least

he isn't scared of dying
since he can't feel fear —

it's a blessing really . . .
She looked away and

smiled, apologizing
for going on like that,

the way my sister did
in her last days each time

the nurse would decompact
her bowels by hand — I'm

sorry, she'd mumble, barely
conscious, sorry, sorry,

till the nurse was through,
her relief, then, less relief

from pain than from the need,
even then, to think of

others. (Didn't we all say
it was so like Beth to do that?)

She could just sleep and
no longer fuel the still

inexorable autonomous
machinery of obligations

that displace us even as
they make us who we are.

Now he was back, her husband,
he smiled when she introduced me,

and before they left for the next
test, next waiting room,

he placed his hand on my shoulder
and said, Good luck, Godspeed,

said it as if he meant it,
as if he could feel it, the gesture

performing itself without him,
like a blinking eyelid

with no eye behind it.
Up on the screen, the crowd

stormed the court in silence
as time expired. My brother

was probably by then
inside a long white

tube where he'd doze while
pictures were being taken

of all the hidden places
in his brain. He was sealed off

and all open, he was free
and confined, and I wanted

him to stay there, where
he didn't have to apologize

to anyone for the delay,
the inconvenience, as

he would to me, as always,
when he returned. I wanted

to sit here and keep watching
the nodding, radiantly

bald head of the color
commentator as he smiled a stiff

smile and held the mike
up high toward the mouth

of the stooping six-ten player
of the game who (I could tell)

was thanking the good Lord
for his God-given this or that.

The Match

O Lord of life,
                bountiful
                        as sunlight
and like the sun
                impartial
                        in your shining
neither kind nor unkind
                        though we call you both
at different moments
                as you flash
                        refracted
through the ever-shifting
                        prism of what happens —
it's you yourself
                you give to
                        when you give
to us —
        yourself
                you show yourself to
                        through us
whenever we're on display
                to one another —
you
    sorting us out
                haphazardly
                        for the
selections
        we think are only
                ours to make.

Who else but you
            could have arranged the scene:
the two boys
            in the hotel pool,
                        the girl
at the pool's edge,
            legs dangling in the water,
all three
            so freshly post-
                        pubescent that
the change itself
            could have been happening
right then
            before us
                        when we stopped to watch,
my brother and I,
            returning to his room
after a day of treatment.
                        We could tell
by how completely
            they ignored her that
their every
            gesture
                        had the girl in mind,
hands locked
            around each other's necks,
                        their fore-
heads touching,

                    water lights
                              and streams of water
running everywhere
                    along their arms,
backs, shoulders,
                    every trembling muscle,
                                        force
requiring counterforce
                    to feel how strong
it is, how irresistible,
                    as now
one quickly slipped down
                    under the other's arm
and groaning
          lifted the twisting
                              torso up
and threw him
          and was on him
                    before the splashes fell.

You neither kind nor unkind,
                    both the end
and means,
          the contest and the prize,
                              the girl
who dipped her calves, her
                    dripping fine-boned ankles
in and out

of the water

        way too non-

chalantly

    to be nonchalant,

        and the boys

who grappled

    in what could

        have been the first

rush of the flowering

    strength inside them

        of you

who were no less

    there

        inside my brother,

no less ferociously

    inside

        each flowering cell

no medicine

    could beat back or slow.

pretty way to describe cancer

Angel of being,

    Proteus,

        who are

    all your

disguises,

    your many forms,

        there is no blessing,

no secret to be

                    wrestled from you,
                                neither
kind nor unkind,
                with magnificent indifference
sorting us out
                to see who best
                            will serve
your riot of good fortune:
                            I had to hold
my brother's arm
                    to keep him steady
while the two boys and girl
                            began to swim
together
            in a circle
                    so we couldn't tell
who was chasing whom.
                        He said he was tired,
he wanted to get
                    back to his room
                                and sleep
before the sickness
                    came on
                            and he woke
entangled in the sheets,
                        drenched,
                                doubled up,
contorted,

   shifting
     all through the long night
from side to side
    as if somehow
       to get
a better grip
   on what he wrestled with.

The Phone Call

The mangled speech, aphasic
pratfalls halfway through the
sentences, the voice
weak, tremulous, taken
by suffering so far
beyond what it once was
it's already otherworldly —
Heracles borne on his litter.

You can't imagine it.

Can't eat, can't drink, can't do a
thing except just lie
in bed before the TV
he's too sick to watch,
one ulcer running down
all the way from lip
to anus like a shirt
of fire burning inside out.

You can't know what it's like.

And even Ellen, sweet Ellen:
her transcendent body just
a torment to him now —
an unignorable
reminder of what he can't
be for her, won't ever be

again, though someone will.
Shirt of fire underneath the skin.

You can't imagine it at all.

What he wants to tell his children
when they call is don't,
you no longer have a father.
The slow annihilation
itself, each agonizing
moment of it now
an eternal labor —
alone on a high crag.

You can't. Don't even try to.

The Accident

While it was happening,
    the absolute
not me of it, the all
    of a sudden see-
through whir of wings beside me
    that the late sun
just as I looked up
    turned to a hovering
flash, a watery gray —
    green iridescence
as the beak dipped into
    a funnel of blossom,
dipped and was gone, and not even
    the blossom's white
tip bent in its going,
    or shivered —

While this, which could have happened
    without me, here
or elsewhere, happened the way
    it did, and would
continue happening
    for others, for no one,
for nothing but the blind urge
    of its happening,
this ever-transient
    accidental
crossing of momentums
    that was, in this case,

beautiful but could
          have not been and so
seemed all the more consoling
          for the thought —

even the thought of death,
          just then, consoling,
shaping itself inside me
          as the now there
now not there hovering
          of bird, flower, late
sun iridescences —
          beloved singers,
you who in the aftermath
          surged from the shadows
to sing in your different voices
          the same song, Route
of evanescence, Mother
          of beauty, It
avails not, time nor place,
          distance avails not,

if you had known, just then,
          three hundred miles
away, in another state,
          that one of the nurses
getting my brother up
          from the commode

and back to bed, the one
    who held him on
his left side, the dead side,
    all of a sudden
lost hold of him and, as
    he fell hard, grabbed
for the loose papery gown
    and ripped it off,
so that he lay there naked,
    utterly exposed —

beloved singers, tricksters
    of solace, if
you had known this, seen
    this, as I did not,
you would have offered him
    no sumptuous
destitution, no fire-
    fangled feathers,
or blab about death as being
    luckier than one
supposes. You would have bowed
    your heads, you would
have silently slipped back
    into the shadows
out of which you surged forth,
    singing to me.

Joy

What never comes when called.

                            What hides when held.

Guest

       most at home where least

                      expected. Vagrant

balm of Gilead.

           What, soon as here,

                   becomes

the body's native ground and,

               soon as not,

its banishment.

          Coming and going,

                indifferent,

magisterial.

        My lovely daughter —

walking me to the car

           to say goodbye

the day I left

       to keep watch at my brother's

bedside —

       suddenly

           singing "I

feel pretty, oh so

       pretty"

         as she raised

her arms up in a loose oval

          over her head

and pirouetted all along the walk.

Savage
        and magisterial —
                        the joy of it,
the animal candor of
                    each arabesque,
each leaping turn and counterturn,
                            her voice
now wobbly
            with laughter,
                        "And I pity
any girl
        who isn't me
                    tonight."
Savagely beautiful,
                not so much like
the lion that the camera
                    freezes
                            in mid-
pounce, claws
            outstretched for the stumbling
                                    antelope,
as like the herd
            escaping
                    that the camera
pans to, zig-
            zagging,
                    swerving as one,
their leaping strides now

leaping higher,
faster,
even after,
it seems,
the fear subsides —
after the fear and
the relief
they keep
on running
for nothing but
the joy of running,
though
it could be
any one of them
is running
from its fallen
mother or father,
sister or brother,
across the wide
savanna,
under a bright sun
into fresher grass.

Up Against

It was your game.
You invented it,
mastered it, played it
undefeatably against me
your little brother
in the evening all
throughout the summer
every summer up
till I was undefeatably
not little anymore.

Up Against, your front-stoop
baseball in which
(at least in memory)
I'm always in "the field,"
out on the street while you,
both batter and pitcher,
lean over the brick
steps, tennis ball
in hand, eye on the point
of the third step which
(if you can hurl the ball
just so against it) will send
the ball high over my head
into the front yard
of the house across from ours.

No joy like the joy
of that, the execution

better than the dream,
sensation of triumph so
extreme you didn't have
to rub it in, the blasé
look of feigned
bewilderment (Gee whiz,
did I do that?) itself
the measure of your exaltation,
and of your need as well
to keep me there so
you could go on playing —

for it was summer,
it would be hours yet
before we're called inside;
summer — and you have just
now made the ball hit
with a sweet whomp
against the brick that
sends it sailing up
and over your brother's out-
stretched hands; have seen,
more sweetly still,
the fury on his face,
the fury and despair.
By God it's summer and
you've cleared the bases.
There's no one out.
The inning could go on forever.

The Last Scene

Extravagant sweep
            of clear sky
                        darkening
in the big picture window
                        beside the bed,
lights here and there
                        already flashing all
across the city down below us —
                        Ellen
and the girls out somewhere,
                        you and I alone,
you with your eyes closed,
                        I with a drink in hand:
you suddenly in character,
                        your voice
a wraith's voice,
            faint, stumbling,
                        slurry
with morphine,
            and yet
                        still artful
                                    as ever,
even if the art
            was obvious,
the dying brother
            playing the dying brother —
Do you think
            you have a problem

with that?

the question

masking a declaration,

the brother

a savior,

the savior a judge,

not all that different from

before except that now

the dying had

distilled

all doubt away

as you repeated,

Do you think

you have a

problem?

"Me? With what?"

I too in character now,

the character

without character,

the little brother who

in your mind proves

the truth

of all you think

by his resistance to it,

pulling

the scene off

by refusing to play it,

pretending not to know:

"With what?"
        With that,
                head tilted to the shot
glass,
      "This?"
            my one desire now
                  a little shtick,
a final moment
           of material —
                  "This?
A problem?
        Not at all.
                There's plenty more
where that came from,
           almost a whole bottle."
You imperturbable,
          Look at yourself,
how you sit here
        drinking all alone.
              "Well, mea
gulpa.
      Are you happy now?"
              You drink
a lot.
      "I have a lot
          to drink about."
And that was that.
        For now you drifted off,

or seemed to,

                your eyes closed,

                                head turned away,

the two of us

         together

                for the last

time ever on the stage

                of being brothers,

our see-through

                figures in the picture window

spectral and vast

             against the city

                    flashing

a ghostly circuitry

            of nerves

                within

the ancient masks we wore,

                the hand I lifted,

the drink I knocked back

             in a final toast

in honor of the timing,

             the concentration

that neither

         one of us

             could ever break.

Fly

Eyes half closed
but flicking
urgently from
side to side
that last long day
as if in search
of some way
out of the dying
body that just
would not die,
as if the body
teased itself
with glimpses of
being rid
of body, the cruel
vision of it
there a moment
above the bed,
then not there, where
is it now? why
won't it keep still?

Eyes half closed,
spasmodic, frantic
as the fly
beside the bed,
the inexhaustible
faint banging
against the window

as it flitted from
side to side, a
tight little knot
of panic on
the glass that teased
it, tortured it,
being at once
the vision of what
the fly so
wanted to get
out into and
the very thing
that kept it
where it was.

The Big Screen

What did it mean, the moaning? Or could you even
call it a moan, what bore no trace of a voice
    we could recognize as his?
Was there even a his by then? Or was it only
a sound, mere sound of the body becoming a thing,
    a spasm, a mere electrical event?
And what about the good hand that, while he moaned,
would move slowly from time to time across
    his forehead, his clenched eyes, his nose—
was it to soothe himself? Did his head still hurt
despite the constant morphine? Or was the gesture
    itself habitual by then,
as automatic as a tic? And when
he wet the bed, and we had to get his shirt off
    and roll him side to side to slip
the clean pad underneath him—as he lay there naked,
what did it mean really when he began
    to sob those dry sobs, infant sobs,
sobs of Can't anyone stop this, can't anyone hear me?
Why won't you do something? And what, too, did
    the fist mean when it rose and shook
as if in protest, as if to say I don't deserve this,
I'll get you you asshole you fucking fuck God—look
    what you did to me! Is that what it was?
Or was it Give me back my body, or
Just get me out of it already, or,
    shivering as the fist shook,
could he have just been cold? And if he was,
was he, by then, even aware of it?

Maybe, as the four of us looked on,
trying to ease him any way we could,
maybe we all along were only sitting
     alone in the same theater in which
from four booths four projectors projected pictures
that were too weak to reach all the way to the screen,
     so that like yarns of light they got
all tangled up in the dark before us while
beyond their tangling ("I think he's . . ." "No,
     no, look, it's got to be . . .") — the screen
stayed blank, the screen of the moaning, the screen
of the dry sobs, of the shaking fist and clenched eyes —
     all of it blank, white, empty,
as if the theater were closed, the seats all upright,
the aisles swept clean, and the four of us somehow there
     too late and too early, before the previews,
after the feature presentation, our eyes
fixed on the big screen nothing flickered on.

Three Questions

What was it like to see him die?

I was thinking how the body,
        mine, not his,
didn't care
        about any of it —
not the hush
around the bedside, not
"the stillness in the air,"
not even my own sorrow —
        it just
went on blindly
        feeding on the food
I'd fed it
                till it
needed more, a furnace
craving fuel,
                        and moved me
to the refrigerator
where I made myself
stare too long
at the refrigerator light
so when I looked
                away
the afterimage
        like a ghostly
pulse appeared
                to hover
    a moment in the air

before my eyes before it failed
 and there was nothing
between the food and me.

Was he ready to die?

In the last moment his eyes
 opened, and the blue
rims of the beautiful
 pale green
irises
 looked toward us as he
all of a sudden rose
on some invisible wave and
 just as suddenly
sank back, and the eyes
stayed open like a doll's
eyes, wide, unblinking,
and the doll was
 in a box inside
a closet in a house
 no one was living in.

Was he at peace?

Like the refrigerator light
after the door is closed.

Broadway Revival

What were my lines?
                The spotlight on my face
made everything pitch-
                black beyond the stage,
invisible.
     Encased in light, I was alone
and looked at.
           The air too thick with heat, too bright.

What were my lines?
                The packed house held its breath.
Who was I playing?
                And why were you there
                              watching
from the wings,
        the script I somehow
                   knew you had
by heart
     splayed
         open in your palm,
one finger pointing
               to the very words
I couldn't
     for the life of me
             remember?

Wasn't this your
            stage, your part,
                   your one

and only
        home, you liked to say, where speech
was song,
        and movement dance and
                        you were most
at ease, a natural,
                most truly who
you were
        when you were someone else?
                                Tell me,
I whispered through clenched
                teeth,
                        tell me my lines.

And did the silence mean
                        you were enjoying this?
Or were we both
                in being there that way
just following another
                        script
                                in which
my lines were
                these, and yours
                        your silence,
                                as if
the theater were itself a stage
                        inside
a theater in which

I play
      the brother
who doesn't know his lines,
          and you the actor
who waits there in the wings,
          who holds the script,
who knows it all
      by heart and
          will not say.

If I Only Knew Then

Let's say you did. Let's
    say there was
a moment half a century ago,

three years before my birth, when you
    had only Beth
and David, and I was, in effect,

where they are now, though my time there,
    of course, would end;
let's say the vision came to you

on a winter night in that back room
    off the kitchen
of the old apartment that you remember

now as an inside pastoral
    retreat; on a night
like any other night in which

the baby's whimpering, his phlegmy
    mews and gurgles,
have awakened Beth, who calls out, Mommy,

Mommy, standing up in her crib,
    shaking the crib bars,
crying, when she sees you go

first to the baby, just as the baby
    too cries when you leave
him to go to Beth. Like every night

you're tired, impatient, angry,
    too indispensable
to stand it, just as you'll later be

unable to stand it when you're not;
    let's say it's then
before you say, Go to sleep already!

Will you just go to sleep, and leave them,
    letting them cry,
not picking them up as all the books say

you mustn't if nobody's sick,
    or wet, or hungry —
let's say it's then that it swoops down on you,

the certainty that you'd outlive them,   *now we're there*
    that one would even
shun you at the end, the vision too

unbearable to believe, too vivid
    to ignore,
as if you were your own Cassandra,

*takes too long to reach that
turning point*

lingering there a little longer,
          rubbing the girl's back,
wrapping the baby tighter in his blanket,

singing them back to sleep this one time
          in a voice less rushed
but still rushing not to get too far

off schedule with these darkening preludes
          about what happens
when the wind blows and the bough breaks.

The Old Man

The day after his son died
all that day
grief was the good mother
                    as he lay in silence
in the bed on his side
knees drawn to chest
hand under cheek
                    eyes open.
Grief was the womb
his posture presupposed;
the absoluteness of it,
                    the encircling
wash of *nothing*
worse than this
can ever happen
                    made it soothing,
peaceful — it seemed
his every feature
was being bathed
                    away until
his face was like a face
before the least
expression scathes it,
                    his eyes the eyes
before the eyelids form,
fish eyes that do not
need to close now
                    not to see.

To the Body

Mutable port of entry, port of call,
cargo and ship —

                    where can we go without you?
Where can we be?

               Anarchic borderland
patrolled by piercing, tattoo, shawl, veil, collar,
earlock and dreadlock;

                    ventriloquist of genes,
vector of history,

          the agonizing

                 stage
on which the anorexic girl performs
clay dreaming spirit dreaming clay;

                 at one
and the same

        time pleasure dome

                   and torture chamber,
prisoner and

         cell and cell

             wall through which
the prisoner taps out

           a message to
the prisoner in the

         next cell who taps his message
back through the wall

          that, separating,

             links.

Even the gods
            and the dead are
                        inconceivable
without you,
            white-vested specter, "tenuous air" —
"But O as to
            embrace me she inclined" —
O bosom of Abraham,
                        the whole world in his hands!
Propitiations
            and provisions all
assume you:
            wine jars, jewels, and
                        honey cakes,
baubles and trinkets
            in the Sun
                        King's tomb,
my addle-brained Aunt Tilly saying,
                        after
the funeral,
            that she just couldn't let
them close the casket till
            she'd placed a golf
ball in her husband's hand
            because my Amos,
you know, he always had
            such a thing
                        for golf;

and yes I mocked her —
                    what did I know about you then? —
I whispered in my
                    brother's ear,
                              Thank God
he didn't have a thing for cottage cheese.
        I mocked her and you took
                         your own
                                   sweet time
to get revenge,
              nearly three decades later
when I saw
          how the embalmers had
                              slicked back
my brother's hair,
                and it wasn't
                        him,
                              it just
wasn't him, and I
              too
                   wouldn't let
them close the casket
                   till I'd tried to palm
the hair down
            over his forehead
                         the way he kept it,
as if the frigid skin would
                    somehow thereby

become less frigid if
                    I got it right.

Death's feedbag, mother lode
                    of yearning, salve
and sore:
                even the worst there is
                            to suffer
seems in my ignorance of it
                    to be no
less precious:
                and though it does no good to ask
you this,
            I ask it anyway:
                        keep me
and those I love
                with you in safety
                            for
a long time yet,
                steer clear of the hidden reef
you also are,
            who are
                    at once the fire
eating the wood
                and the wood that,
                            burning,
                    eats the fire.

Song and Dance

Did you ever have a family?
                                  Dark
dining room,
                        bright kitchen,
                                              white steam
from the big pot my mother's stirring
reaching in wavy tendrils to her face,
around her face, all the way around
to me at the table, then beyond me
into the darkness where my brother is.

Were you ever a child?
                              I'm hungry
but I know we'll
                        eat soon,
                                          so
even the hunger's sweet.

Did you ever really have a brother?
                                  He's singing
there in the dark
                        corner
                              beside the stereo,
the volume turned down so low
all we hear is him, his voice, and
his eyes are closed so that there's
nothing around him anywhere
that might reveal he isn't
who the song insists he is.

And that is?

Irresistible,

unforgettable,

someone

to whom

as in imaginary gardens
where "the nectarine and curious
peach into my hands themselves
do reach," love comes as soon
as called, comes just as dreamed.

Did any of this ever happen?

The hunger's

sweet,

it's as if

the song weaves

through the fragrance of the braiding
steam from him to me to her
to me to him because her eyes
are closed now too; her
slippered feet tap, caper
a soft shoe while the ladle
sways in her hand as she stirs.

Were you ever a child?

I know

I'll eat soon.

Did you ever really have a brother?

You should have

                    heard him,
                                    his voice was
unforgettable, irresistible, his voice
was an imaginary garden
woven through with fragrance.

Did you ever have a family?
                                Their eyes are closed.
That's how I know
                    we're there
                                    inside it,
it's made of sound and steam
that weaves between dark
dining room, bright kitchen.
We're there because I'm hungry,
and we'll all be eating soon
together, and the hunger's sweet.

Last Impressions

When the doctor asked you, "If we deem it necessary to perform the surgery, will you be able to afford the operation?" you held up one talmudic finger à la Jackie Mason as you answered, "And if I can't afford the operation, will you deem it necessary to perform the surgery?"

And after the surgery, the Groucho Marx you whispered in my ear when the neurosurgeon, grim as an accountant, though without the personality, presented the two paths of treatment you could take — do nothing and live pretty well (little or no "premorbidity" is how he put it) until the end or go the standard route of chemo/radiation and be very sick but increase the odds of living more than a year from zero to one percent — your voice so perfect I could smell the smoke from the invisible cigar you held between two fingers as you whispered, "It's like having to choose your favorite Menendez brother."

On the eve of your second surgery, your invention of the James Brown Alarm Clock that goes off, shouting, "Help me now! Help me! Help me!"

The Jimmy Cagney you reserved exclusively for the examination room, where the two of us would wait sometimes for hours for the doctor to arrive with the MRI results; you pacing in that room that was hardly bigger than a closet, agitated, cursing, unreachable inside your mounting panic, and when you finally had had enough and opened the door and stood there in the doorway looking out at the doctors, nurses, patients bustling to and fro, you'd catch a nurse's eye and suddenly Cagney, holding on to imaginary prison bars, would ask, "Any news from the governor?"

The freakish taffy of your face doing Crazy Guggenheim whenever my kids would call, the lower jaw askew, the mouth wrenched sideways, only the corner of it moving as the exuberant dumb voice says, "Hiya Joe, hiya Mista Dunahee-hee-hee."

Or later, toward the end, your Bette Davis, when the nurse would ask you every morning how the paralyzed left arm was doing: "Dead," you'd say, the right hand lifting up the left, the furtive breathiness between the *d*'s just right, the nurse who knew what to expect by then still cracking up when you say it twice more, "Dead. Dead," before you let the hand go and it falls like someone else's hand back to the bed.

Comedy, from the Greek *komoidia,* out of *komoidos* — *komos* meaning revel, and *oidos,* singer. The comic, then, is the singer in the revels.

So if your cancer was the gravity that pulled you every moment down into the isolating black hole of your dying, could the impressions, comebacks, quips, the little shuffle-off-to-Buffaloes you'd do for the nurses after each examination, even after the last one — two days later you'd be paralyzed — could all that comedy have been the grace that kept you here among us where you could go on being the comedian, the singer in the revels, joking as if your life depended on it?

But where's the rage in that? The rage that ran through all the voices, all the manic shtick, the refusal not to be funny — "Death, where is thy sting-a-ling?" — as if the cancer wanted all the jokes to end, as if the cancer weren't a random spin of the genetic wheel, a biochemical mishap run amuck, absurd for its impersonality, but a character from Central Casting, Uriah Heep or Scrooge, or worse in your pantheon of villains, a puckerbutted Pooh-Bah in a white tuxedo on a busy corner hailing a cab, and your Jerry Lewis's "LAAAADY" or your Arnold Schwarzenegger's "Dis is not a tuma!" is the cab that doesn't stop but roars by through a puddle that sprays the immaculate white suit black with muck?

middle finger to the cancer

© John Rosenthal

Alan Shapiro is the author of many books of poetry,
including *The Dead Alive and Busy,* winner of the 2001
Kingsley Tufts Award. His collection *Mixed Company*
won the Los Angeles Times Book Prize, and his
memoir, *The Last Happy Occasion,* was a finalist for
the National Book Critics Circle Award. The recipi-
ent of an American Academy of Arts and Letters
Award in Literature, he teaches at the University of
North Carolina at Chapel Hill.

CPSIA information can be obtained
at www.ICGtesting.com
Printed in the USA
LVOW12s1529151216
517423LV00002B/339/P